Ancient
GREECE

Peter Connolly

OXFORD

Ancient
GREECE

Peter Connolly

text by Andrew Solway

OXFORD
UNIVERSITY PRESS

OXFORD
UNIVERSITY PRESS

Great Clarendon Street, Oxford OX2 6DP

Oxford University Press is a department of the University of Oxford.
It furthers the University's objective of excellence in research, scholarship,
and education by publishing worldwide in

Oxford New York

Athens Auckland Bangkok Bogotá Buenos Aires Calcutta
Cape Town Chennai Dar es Salaam Delhi Florence Hong Kong Istanbul
Karachi Kuala Lumpur Madrid Melbourne Mexico City Mumbai
Nairobi Paris São Paulo Shanghai Singapore Taipei Tokyo Toronto Warsaw

with associated companies in Berlin Ibadan

Oxford is a registered trade mark of Oxford University Press
in the UK and in certain other countries

British Library Cataloguing in Publication Data available

Hardback ISBN 0-19-910810-2

1 3 5 7 9 10 8 6 4 2

Printed in Hong Kong

C
9 38
SOWW 09/01

500 615208

Contents

Athens

Between 500 and 400 BC, Greece was the most advanced culture in the ancient world. And Athens was the greatest city in Greece. Some of the best artists, writers, leaders and thinkers in history lived in this one city.

Athens was also the home of the first democracy. This meant that all the citizens in Athens met together regularly, to decide how the city should be run. Not everyone in Athens was a citizen. Women could not vote, nor could foreigners or slaves. But it would be over 2000 years before any other city gave so many of its citizens a vote.

▶ The Acropolis, the hill at the centre of Athens, was the site of the city's main temples. The largest building on the Acropolis was the Parthenon, a temple to the goddess Athena.

▼ Athens, Corinth and Sparta were the main cities in Greece, but there were many others. Greek colonies were scattered across the Mediterranean, from Spain to the Black Sea.

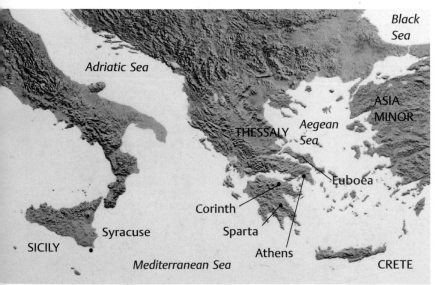

Adriatic Sea

Black Sea

ASIA MINOR

Aegean Sea

THESSALY

Euboea

Corinth

Sparta

Syracuse

SICILY

Athens

Mediterranean Sea

CRETE

Athens, Sparta and Persia

Ancient Greece was not one country, with a single ruler or government. It was a collection of small states, each of them a city and its surrounding countryside. There were also hundreds of island states, and small Greek colonies in other parts of the Mediterranean. At times these states would join together for strength, or to fight off an invader. But just as often, they fought among themselves.

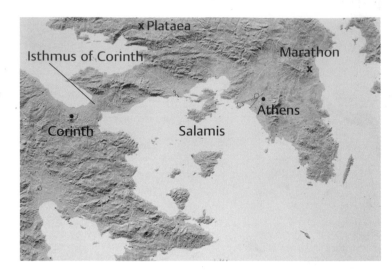

▼ An Athenian war galley, or trireme. The front of the ship was a battering ram. Three rows of rowers drove the ram with tremendous force into the side of an enemy boat.

▲ This map shows where the main battles with the Persians took place. (Thermopylae is far to the north of the map area.)

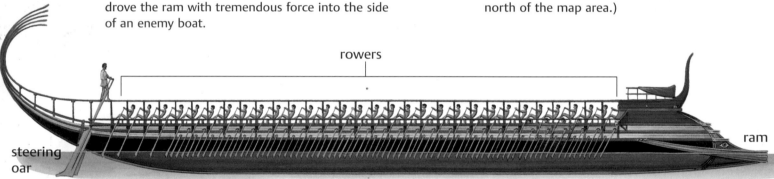

rowers

steering oar

ram

Athens and Sparta

The two most powerful Greek nations were Athens and Sparta. The Spartans lived in southern Greece. Their soldiers were tremendous fighters, and the Spartan army had conquered many neighbouring states. The country was ruled by two kings, who were also the army commanders.

Athens was a strong sea power. It had a fleet of fast galleys called triremes that were the most advanced fighting ships of their time. Athens was at first ruled by nine leaders called archons. But by the 5th century BC the archons had lost power. Decisions were made by an Assembly, in which all male citizens over 18 could take part.

Persia invades

East of Greece was the huge Persian empire. Some Greek colonies in Asia Minor were conquered by the Persians, and Athens tried to help these colonies become independent once more. This angered the Persians, who sent an army to invade Athens. But the Athenians defeated the Persians at Marathon.

The Athenians knew that this was not the end of the fighting, and they asked the other Greek nations for help. Soon a much bigger Persian army arrived, led by the Persian king Xerxes himself. A small Spartan army made a heroic attempt to stop the Persians at Thermopylae. But the Persians burst through, and marched into Athens.

Salamis and Plataea

The capture of Athens was a great blow. But most Athenians had fled the city, and the Greek army and navy were intact. The Persians found that they could not get past the Greek army in the narrow Isthmus of Corinth. The only way into the rest of Greece was by sea. Xerxes had a strong navy, and was confident of victory. But the Greek navy was led by the wily Athenian commander, Themistocles. He lured the Persians into the narrow channel between the island of Salamis and mainland Greece, where the Greek triremes destroyed many Persian ships in a tremendous battle.

After this defeat Xerxes went home, leaving his army under the command of general Mardonius. But the Greeks were no longer frightened by the huge Persian army. A year later, in 479 BC, they defeated the Persians and killed Mardonius at Plataea.

► A Spartan soldier. All Spartan boys trained as soldiers from the age of seven, and served in the army until they were 59. They were expected to stand the most severe beatings without showing pain.

▼ Athenians (left) and Persians fighting at the battle of Marathon. Over 6000 Persian soldiers were killed, while Athens lost only 200 men.

9

New defences

After the Persian invasion, Athens was left in ruins. The whole city was destroyed – hardly a building was left standing. The Athenians did not immediately rebuild the burnt temples and shrines. These lay in ruins for over 30 years, to remind them what the Persians had done to their city. The Athenians concentrated on making their city safe from any further attacks. They began by building a strong defensive wall all around the city.

▲ The Acropolis in about 480 BC, just before the Persian invasion. The Athenians were already working on a new temple to Athena, but all their work was destroyed when the Persians took the city.

Diplyon
Gate

Sacred
Gate

▲ The Diplyon Gate was the main gate into Athens. Next to it was the slightly smaller Sacred Gate. The Eridanus River ran out of the city by the side of the Sacred Gate.

Towers and gates

The new city wall was built of mud brick and plaster, on a strong stone foundation. It was about $2\frac{1}{2}$ metres thick and 7 or 8 metres high. The wall was strengthened every so often by square towers. There were 15 large gates in the wall. Each was protected by two towers, and the most important were set back from the main wall. This meant that an enemy army trying to get in would be surrounded on three sides as they approached.

The long walls

Once the walls around the city were completed, the Athenians went on to build two more long walls, running either side of the road from Athens to the port of Piraeus, about 5 kilometres away. If Athens were besieged, it would be vital to keep open this route to the sea.

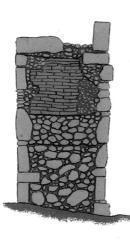

◀ The city walls were rebuilt several times before they eventually fell into ruin. This cross-section through a piece of wall that is still standing shows how the original mud brick wall formed a filling for later stone foundations.

▶ A small section of the city wall, showing the stone foundation with mud brick above. The mud bricks were covered over with a layer of plaster.

11

Ships

Athens was a trading state. Attica, the region surrounding Athens, grew olives for olive oil and grapes to make wine. There was an important silver mine at Laurium, near Athens, and the city was famous for its pottery. All these products were sold abroad in return for essential food supplies – in particular, wheat grain. Merchant ships brought wheat grain from the nearby island of Euboea and the rich farmlands around the Black Sea. One of the main reasons Athens needed a strong navy was to protect this merchant fleet.

Piraeus

Both the merchant ships and the navy's triremes needed a safe harbour. The port of Piraeus, just outside Athens, had three excellent natural harbours. The largest was Kantharos, to the north, with two smaller harbours, Munichia and Zea, to the south. Zea was the main naval harbour. Soon after the Persian defeat, all three harbours were made safer from attack. Walls were built out into the sea, almost closing off the harbour entrance. Only a small entrance was left, and this could be closed off with chains.

▼ This reconstruction of a sea battle shows Athenian triremes in action. The trireme in the foreground is ramming an enemy ship in the side, smashing its oars in the process.

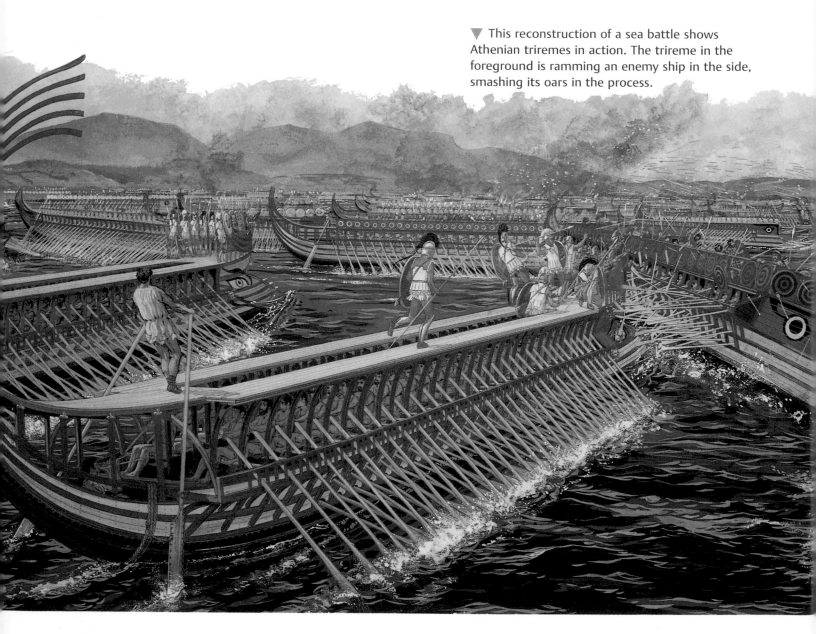

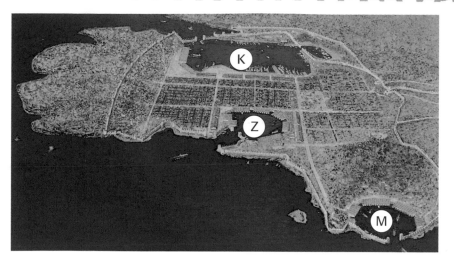

The port of Piraeus as it might have looked in about 430 BC. In the foreground is Munichia (M), with Zea (Z) in the centre and Kantharos (K) at the top of the picture.

A reconstruction of how the Athenian ship sheds might have looked. Each shed was actually a slipway, so that ships could be quickly launched into the water.

Ship sheds

During the winter months, seas were too rough for warships to operate. They were therefore stored away in long sheds, to keep them safe from the weather and from enemy attack. There were nearly 200 ship sheds around Zea harbour, over 80 at Munichia and over 90 at Kantharos. There were also large storehouses at the harbours for ships' cables, sails and other equipment.

The painting on this bowl shows a ship under sail. Triremes used sails when they were not actually fighting. Merchant ships had fewer rowers and relied more on sail-power.

Daily life

Life in Athens was very different for men and women, the rich and poor, free citizens and slaves. Only wealthy Athenian men could really enjoy the freedom and cultural life that the city could offer. Women were expected to spend almost all their time looking after the home and the children, while slaves had no freedom at all – they were at the command of their masters.

▲ A toy chariot found in Athens. It is made from terracotta, a kind of pottery.

A new birth

Athenians did not have large families. Boys were valued much more than girls. Girls also had the disadvantage of needing a dowry (money paid to the bridegroom's family) when they married. Unwanted babies were left out in the open to die: this was not a crime in Athens. Sometimes a family who could not have children would rescue an unwanted baby.

When a new child was born, its father proclaimed the birth by hanging an olive branch by the front door. About ten days after the birth there was a celebratory meal, and the family gave presents to the new baby. Poor women had to care for their own children, but many mothers had a slave to help nurse the baby.

◀ This vase painting shows a mother with her baby. The baby is sitting in a high chair. A similar high chair, made of terracotta, was found in the Athenian marketplace by archaeologists.

▼ A baby's feeding bottle. This is also made from terracotta, glazed black.

Childhood games

Until the age of about 7, boys and girls were brought up at home. They played with dolls and balls, and may even have had a toy chariot to ride in. Mothers would tell their children stories and rhymes – they would for example have known Aesop's fables, stories about animals that you can still read today. After the age of about 7, girls began to help around the house – but boys were sent to school.

▲ This vase painting shows an Athenian boy rolling a hoop.

School

All but the poorest boys in Athens went to school from about 7 years old. They were put in the charge of a slave, known as a *paidotribes*, who took them to and from school, tested them on their work, and made sure they behaved. School was held in the house of the teacher. Boys learned to read and write, and to do arithmetic. They learned history from Greek writers. And as they got older, they learned to sing and play the lyre or flute.

▼ Another vase painting, this time showing two boys at school. One is learning the lyre, the other is reading from a scroll.

▶ Two young men wrestling. The man with the long, two-branched stick is the teacher, or *paidotribes*.

▼ This young woman is playing the *cithara*, a kind of small lyre.

Physical training

From about the age of 12, exercise and physical education became the most important part of a boy's schooling. The boys took off their clothes to exercise, sprinkling themselves with dust or fine sand to keep off chills. Then they went to an open space called the gymnasium, where they would wrestle, do gymnastics, and sports such as running, jumping and throwing the javelin. After exercise the boys would wash at the bath house before dressing.

Education for girls

Athenian girls did not go to school. However, in richer families they might have a tutor at home, who would teach them to read and write, and to play music and sing. Athenian girls did not take part in sports and exercises like the boys. Spartan girls, in contrast, did exercise in public. This was very shocking to Athenians.

▲ A bronze breastplate, or cuirass. Only the richer Athenians could afford this kind of body armour.

▶ A hoplite is putting on his armour. He is wearing a cuirass made out of layers of linen, and bronze greaves to protect his legs. He also has a bronze helmet and a large round shield.

Military service

All Athenian men were obliged to serve in the army in times of war. So when boys finished school at 18, they went on to do two years of military training. Soldiers were called hoplites. Each man had to provide his own equipment and food. For protection, hoplites wore a helmet and carried a round shield. Their main weapons were a spear and a sword.

Athenians and Spartans fought in a formation called a phalanx. The phalanx was a long line, four to eight rows deep. The soldiers carried long spears, and those in the first two rows could thrust at the enemy. The soldiers in the rows behind were ready to step in and fill the gap if one of the men in front fell.

Clothing

Greeks did not wear complicated garments made from shaped pieces of cloth sewn together. Their basic garment was a tunic, made from two rectangular pieces of cloth. Most commonly, clothing was made from woollen cloth, but linen was also used (for example for hoplite armour). Clothing for the poor was made from a very coarse cloth made from animal hair.

Men's clothes

Men wore a short tunic, called a *chiton*. Over this, they wore a large piece of woollen cloth called a *himation*. This was wrapped around the body, and in cold weather could be pulled over the head. Soldiers often wore a cloak made from thicker cloth, called a *chlamys*. This was fastened at the neck with a clasp. Boys usually went barefoot in summer, but men wore shoes. These ranged from light sandals to sturdy boots.

▲ The man on the left is wearing a *himation*, boots and a felt hat. The man on the right is wearing a tunic and sandals.

▼ Typical hairstyles for men.

Hairstyles

Men could wear their hair short or long. Young men were usually clean-shaven, but older men are usually shown with beards. Women wore their hair long, often pulled back into a pony tail or a bun. Women often wore ribbons and head scarves in their hair.

◄ Different kinds of men's clothing shown on vase paintings. The top figure wears an elaborate *chiton*; the figure below has folded the top of his tunic down. The three central figures are wearing a *himation*, and one has it pulled over his head. The bottom figure is wearing a heavy cloak or *chlamys*.

18

◀ The woman on the left is wearing a long tunic fastened at the shoulders and waist. The other two women wear a *himation* over their tunic.

Women's clothes

Women wore a longer tunic reaching down to their ankles. Sometimes the tunic was simply tailored, like the men's, but more elaborate tunics had sleeves and were fastened at the waist and the hips. Like men, women wore a *himation* over this tunic. Pictures of women rarely show them wearing shoes, but they did wear light sandals.

▶ Pictures of women's clothing from vase paintings. The top woman is wearing the coarse Doric tunic worn by Spartan women. The two women below her are wearing lighter tunics, which were more popular in Athens. The four women below this are wearing the *himation* in various ways.

▼ Three examples of women's hairstyles.

Women's work

Athenian women led very restricted lives. They were expected to spend most of their time in the home, looking after the house and the younger children, preparing and cooking the meals, and spinning and weaving cloth. In richer homes, however, many of these jobs were done by slaves. Women did not go out with their husbands. They did not even eat with the other guests if their husband held a dinner party. However, they were not forbidden to go out altogether. Women who had the leisure time would visit the homes of friends, or go out to the theatre. There were also religious festivals and athletics meetings that were specifically for women.

▲ Women needed to know every stage of making cloth from raw wool. The seated woman in this picture is rolling the cleaned and combed wool on her leg in preparation for spinning it.

▼ Another scene from home life shows two women and a girl airing clothes over a fire.

20

A slave carrying two large jars, or amphorae, probably full of water.

Slavery and freedom

All Athenians who could afford it had slaves. Only the poorest families had no slaves at all. Most slaves were people captured in foreign wars. Slaves did all the most unpleasant jobs – for example, the silver mines near Athens were dug by slaves. But slaves who were skilled or well-educated often had more pleasant jobs, for example as potters, painters or secretaries. Slaves could be granted their freedom by their masters, for outstanding or long service. But even as freedmen and women they did not have the same rights as Athenian citizens: for example, they were not allowed to vote in the Assembly.

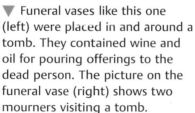

Funeral vases like this one (left) were placed in and around a tomb. They contained wine and oil for pouring offerings to the dead person. The picture on the funeral vase (right) shows two mourners visiting a tomb.

Old age and death

Old people were respected for their wisdom, and cared for by their children. When someone died, they were bound in waxed cloths and put in a coffin. The coffin stayed in the house for a day before the funeral. Then it was carried in a funeral procession to the family burial ground. There the body would either be cremated (burned) or buried.

▼ This bowl on a high stand was called a *lebes gamikos*. They were made especially for weddings.

Getting married

An Athenian girl married at the age of 14 or 15. She had no say about who she married. Marriages were arranged between the groom and the father of the bride.

Getting married was an important step for a girl. Until then she would have known little more than her home and her family. On the day before the wedding, the bride made a sacrifice to one of the wedding gods: Hera, Zeus, Artemis or Apollo. Her favourite dolls, clothes and toys were burnt on the altar as an offering to the god. After this ceremony the girl took a bridal bath. At his house, the groom also bathed on the eve of his wedding.

▶ The wedding procession leaves the bride's house. The groom is just climbing into the wedding chariot beside the bride. Two figures carry torches: the others are carrying wedding presents.

◄ This painting shows a bride surrounded by friends and relations bringing wedding presents. Winged spirits called *erotes* fly among the guests. The woman fourth from the left in the picture is carrying a wedding bowl on a tall stand, similar to the one shown below.

The wedding day

At the bride's house, the morning was spent preparing a wedding feast. The bride dressed in her best clothes and put on a veil, crowned with a wreath of leaves. In the afternoon, the groom arrived at the house with his family and the best man. First there was a sacrifice to the gods, then everyone sat down to the feast. The men sat separately from the women. After the meal the wedding guests gave the new couple their presents. As night fell, the father of the bride gave his daughter to the groom.

The procession

Now everyone got ready for a procession from the bride's home to the groom's. At the front went the *progetes*, the procession leader. Behind him came the newly married couple in a chariot, or open carriage, and the other guests carrying torches and the wedding gifts. As they walked, the guests sang the marriage hymn. At the door of the groom's house the couple were met by the groom's parents, and the wedding guests showered the bride with nuts and figs. As the couple entered the house, the guests sang as noisily as possible to ward off evil spirits.

Houses

The streets of Athens were mostly narrow and winding, and the city was not laid out according to any plan. Houses had no front gardens, which made the streets seem even narrower. The only really broad road was the Panathenaic Way, leading from the Diplyon Gate to the Acropolis. Streets had good drainage, however, and were regularly swept by groups of slaves. As in any city there were all kinds of houses, from spacious mansions to tiny huts.

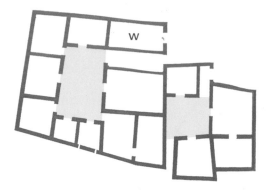

▲ A plan of the semi-detached houses shown below. The courtyard in each house is shaded. The room that might have been a workshop is marked 'w'.

Athenian houses

Many ancient Athenian houses have been dug up by archaeologists. Most are only foundations, but by looking at many different examples, it has been possible to get an idea of what the houses looked like. Most had walls made of mud-brick and plaster, with a gently sloping roof covered with either tiles or thatch. Most houses were built around a central courtyard.

▲ A reconstruction of two semi-detached houses. At least part of each house has a second storey, and a balcony overlooking the courtyard.

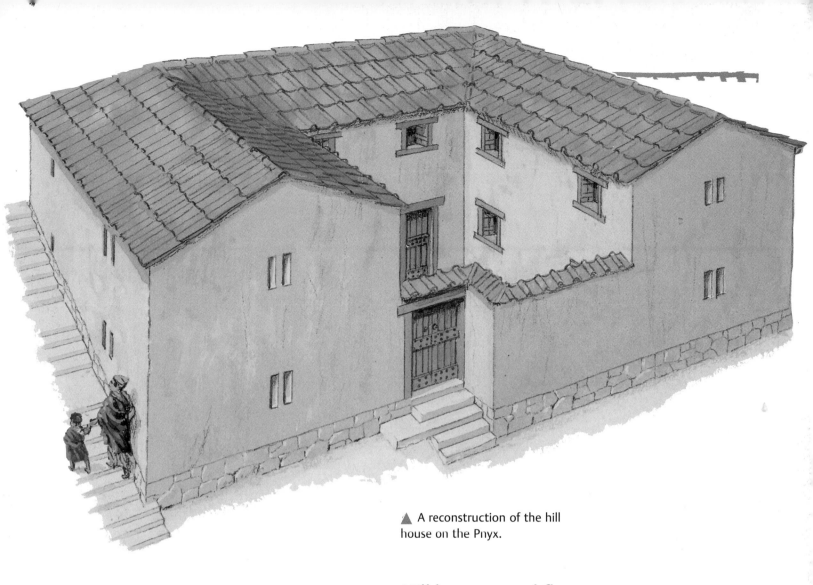

▲ A reconstruction of the hill house on the Pnyx.

Hill houses and flats

Another type of house was found on the Pnyx, a hill close to the centre of Athens. The house was set into the hillside, and the ground-floor rooms were half underground. This house also has a courtyard, with rooms on three sides. Another excavation has found a block of six houses, each with its own courtyard. All these houses seem to have had an upper floor.

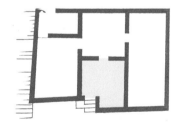

▶ A plan of the hill house. The shaded area is the courtyard.

Semi-detached houses

One building that has been found was made up of two semi-detached houses. The doors and windows of both houses faced on to a central courtyard; there were no windows looking out into the street. An unusual room in the larger house had no connection to the house itself – the only way in was from the street. This room was probably a workshop.

▶ This bronze door knocker was found on the site of another house. A similar knocker may have been fitted on the door of the hill house.

25

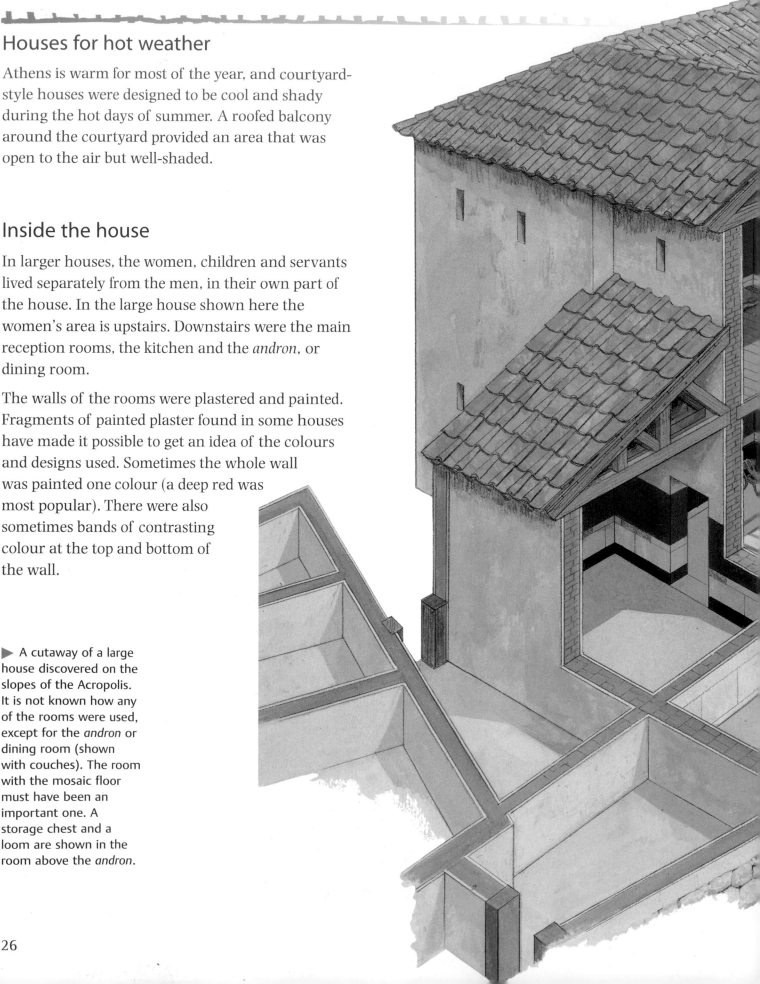

Houses for hot weather

Athens is warm for most of the year, and courtyard-style houses were designed to be cool and shady during the hot days of summer. A roofed balcony around the courtyard provided an area that was open to the air but well-shaded.

Inside the house

In larger houses, the women, children and servants lived separately from the men, in their own part of the house. In the large house shown here the women's area is upstairs. Downstairs were the main reception rooms, the kitchen and the *andron*, or dining room.

The walls of the rooms were plastered and painted. Fragments of painted plaster found in some houses have made it possible to get an idea of the colours and designs used. Sometimes the whole wall was painted one colour (a deep red was most popular). There were also sometimes bands of contrasting colour at the top and bottom of the wall.

▶ A cutaway of a large house discovered on the slopes of the Acropolis. It is not known how any of the rooms were used, except for the *andron* or dining room (shown with couches). The room with the mosaic floor must have been an important one. A storage chest and a loom are shown in the room above the *andron*.

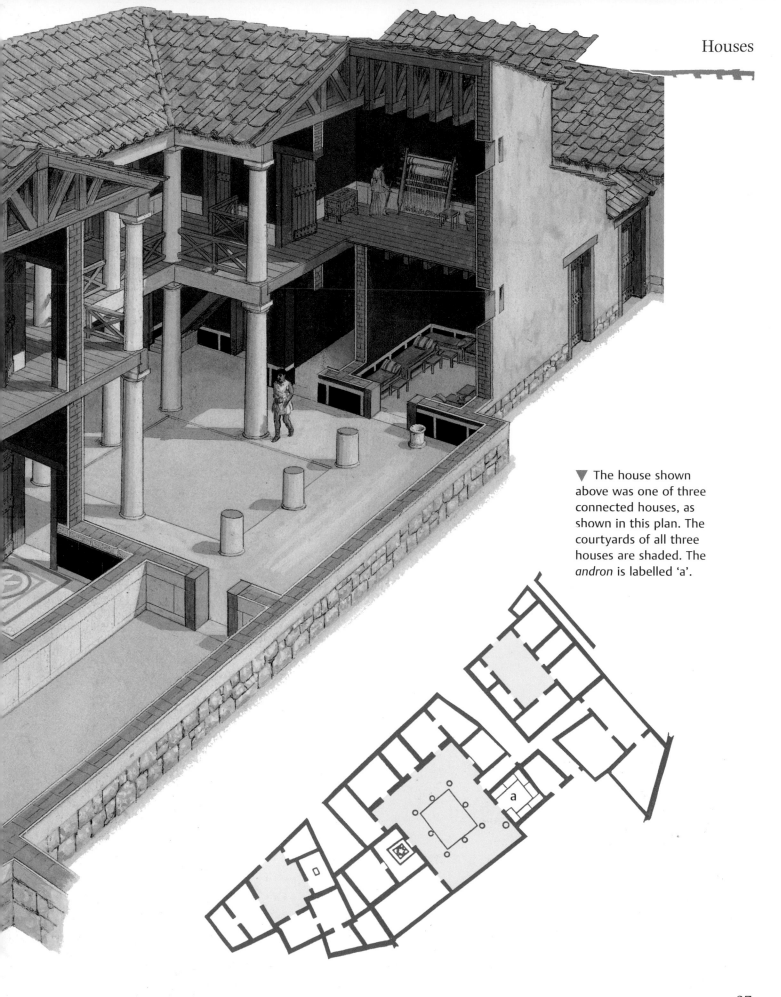

▼ The house shown above was one of three connected houses, as shown in this plan. The courtyards of all three houses are shaded. The *andron* is labelled 'a'.

a

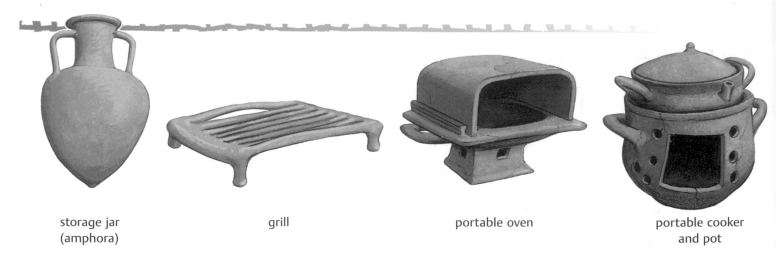

storage jar
(amphora)

grill

portable oven

portable cooker
and pot

▲ Kitchen equipment made of terracotta from
Athens in the 5th century BC.

The dining room

The dining room or *andron* was used at meal times,
but also when entertaining guests (see page 50).
Because it was an important entertaining room, the
floor was often decorated with an elaborate mosaic.
At normal meal times the family would all eat there.
Women and children sat on stools or chairs, but men
reclined on couches to eat. The room had a slightly
raised area around the edge on which couches could
be placed. Food was served in bowls on small tables.
Most food was eaten with the fingers.

The kitchen

Archaeologists have found hearths in the rooms of
some houses – these may have been kitchens. The
kitchen was usually next to the dining room.

Athenians cooked over an open fire. The food they
ate was usually quite simple, and most cooking was
done using a cooking pot hung from a tripod. Bread
was served with every meal, and this was baked in
a clay oven. Grills were used to cook such foods as
sausages and fish, but meat and fish were not
often part of the meal for most Athenians.

◀ This statuette from the 6th century BC shows a
woman making bread. Rather than mixing the
ingredients in a bowl, she is using a large baking
trough.

Bathrooms and toilets

In some houses a small area close to the kitchen was used as a bathroom. This had a small hip bath in it. Vase paintings also show women washing at waist-high basins, or using a simple shower arrangement. There were no taps, and no hot water. Water had to be heated in a large pot over the fire, then poured into the bath or basin.

Most houses had some form of toilet – usually a seat and a bucket. Children used a chamber pot.

Furniture

Athenian houses had relatively little furniture. It was usually made of wood, with criss-crossed straps of webbing for the seats of chairs and the bases of couches. Tables, chairs, stools and couches were moved from room to room as they were needed. Clothes and bed linen were kept in chests, scented with dried fruits or herbs. There were vases in many rooms, especially the elegant *lebes gamikos* vases given at weddings. Houses were lit with oil lamps, and in winter braziers kept the rooms warm.

▶ Some Athenian furniture from vase paintings. In the centre are a dining couch and table.

▼ A child's potty, or chamber pot (top), and a toilet seat.

Religion

The ancient Greeks had many gods. The most important of these were the Olympians, the great gods who were believed to live on Mount Olympus. But there were many other lesser gods, spirits and god-like heroes.

The Olympians

The leader of all the Greek gods was Zeus. He was lord of the sky, and controlled the weather. His wife, Hera, was the goddess of marriage. Zeus had two brothers: Poseidon, who controlled the sea, and Hades, ruler of the underworld (the land of the dead). No god ruled the earth, which was the province of humans. The other gods were Apollo, the sun god (god of music and prophecy), his twin sister Artemis (goddess of hunting and nature), Demeter (goddess of the harvest and fertility), Athena (goddess of wisdom and war), Hephaestus (god of metalwork and fire), Aphrodite (goddess of love), Ares (god of war) and Hermes, the gods' messenger.

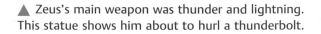

▲ Zeus's main weapon was thunder and lightning. This statue shows him about to hurl a thunderbolt.

Athena

Although Zeus was head of the gods, each city or area had one god that was special to them. Athens was named after the goddess Athena. There were many temples to Athena, including the Parthenon temple on the Acropolis. Athena was a daughter of Zeus. Greek legends say that she was not born in the normal way, but sprang fully armed from Zeus's forehead. The owl was sacred to Athena, and was a symbol of wisdom.

▶ A reconstruction of the huge statue of Athena in the Parthenon. Athena wears a helmet and carries a shield. The winged goddess Victory is on her right palm. Behind her shield is a snake, another symbol of wisdom.

◀ A worshipper at the temple of Apollo. Apollo himself sits on a throne in the temple. The rounded object in front of him is the *omphalos* – the centre of the world.

Temples

A temple was not a place where people regularly worshipped. The building was built to house a statue or other image of the god: it was the god's 'house'. People would go to the temple to ask the god for his or her favour. Often they would leave a small offering of food. The size of the temple building was a measure of the importance of the god in that city or community. Sacrifices were not made inside the temple, but at an altar or shrine outside it.

Sacrifices

Throughout the year there were festivals to different gods. The festival began with a procession, with music and singing, in which an animal to be sacrificed was led through the streets. The procession ended at the altar, which was outside the god's temple. The priest killed the animal on the altar, and parts of it were burned as an offering to the gods. The rest of the meat was cooked as a feast for the people at the festival.

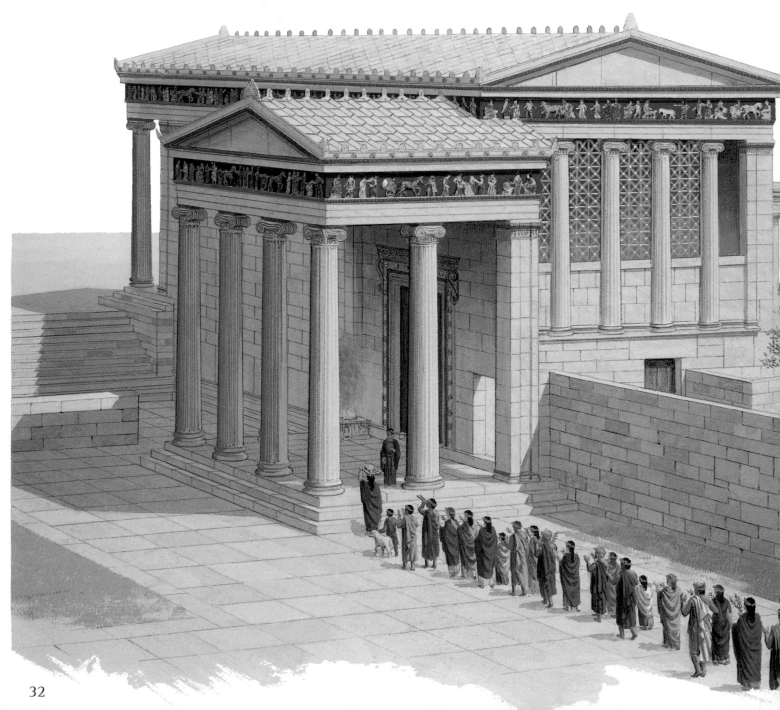

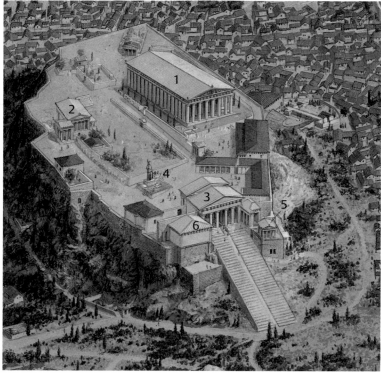

▼ The Erectheum, one of the temples on the Acropolis, was really two temples, each containing tombs and sites sacred to different gods or heroes. It was named after Erectheus, a legendary hero who was the first king of Athens.

▲ The main temples and other buildings on the Acropolis.

1   Parthenon (temple of Athena Parthenos)
2   Erectheum (temple to several gods)
3   Propylaea (entrance way)
4   Bronze statue of Athena
5   Temple of Nike (Victory)
6   Pinakotheke (picture gallery)

Rebuilding the Acropolis

In the middle of the 5th century BC, Athens and Persia agreed a peace treaty. The Acropolis had been in ruins for 30 years, but with the swearing of the treaty the soldier and statesman Pericles persuaded the Athenian Assembly that it was time to rebuild. Work began in 447 BC on the first building – the temple to Athena Parthenos, now known simply as the Parthenon. Other buildings were begun soon afterwards – the Propylaea, the gateway to the Acropolis, in 437 BC, and the Erectheum around 420 BC.

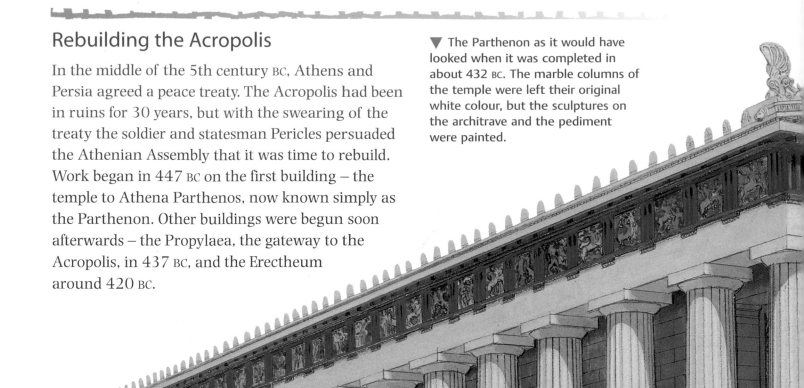

▼ The Parthenon as it would have looked when it was completed in about 432 BC. The marble columns of the temple were left their original white colour, but the sculptures on the architrave and the pediment were painted.

The Parthenon

The Parthenon was designed by the great sculptor Phidias. The general design of the temple was traditional, similar to temples all over ancient Greece. But the size of the building, the superb sculptures which decorated it and the details of its design made the Parthenon one of the most beautiful and famous buildings in the world.

The Parthenon survived almost intact for over 2000 years, becoming at one point a church and then a Turkish mosque. But in 1687 the Venetians besieged Athens, and their cannons bombarded the city. A gunpowder store in the Parthenon was hit by gunfire, there was an explosion, and the centre of the temple was blown out.

pediment

architrave

columns

▶ These three figures are from the sculpture that was on the east pediment of the Parthenon. Parts of these figures can be seen in the British Museum in London. The colour scheme of this reconstruction is based on tiny traces of paint found on the sculptures.

Building begins

The Parthenon was built mostly from white marble from Mount Pentelicon, to the north-east of Athens. The first part to be built was the outer colonnade. Each column was made up of 11 separate pieces. The inner chamber, or *cella*, was constructed from stone blocks, held together with metal clamps. Inside the *cella* was the huge statue of Athena (see page 31).

▲ The Parthenon as it looks today. The roof, the inner building and the main sculptures have all been either destroyed or removed.

▼ A cutaway showing the inner structure of the Parthenon. A continuous band of sculpture, the Panathenaic Frieze, ran around the top of the inner building, or *cella*. The statue of Athena can just be seen between the inner columns.

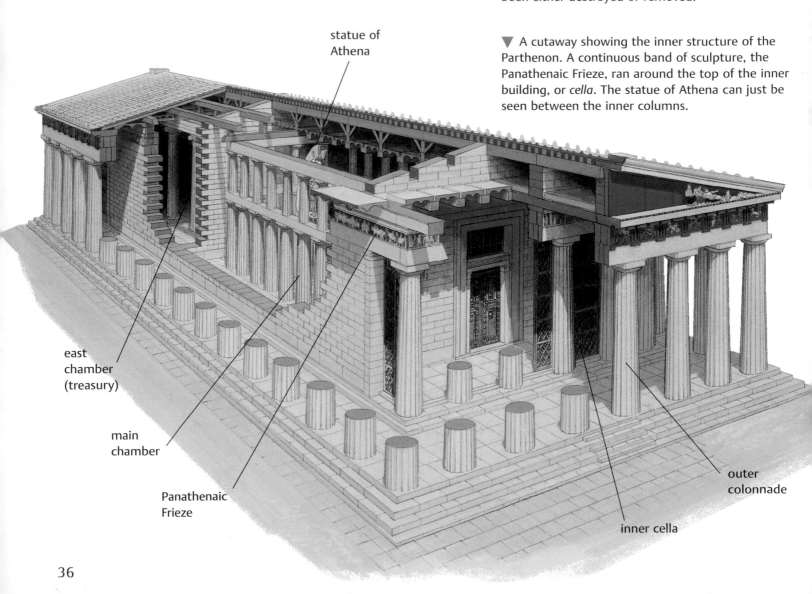

statue of Athena

east chamber (treasury)

main chamber

Panathenaic Frieze

inner cella

outer colonnade

36

Skill and ingenuity

Most of the work on the Parthenon was done using simple tools, together with an enormous amount of skill and ingenuity. For example, small projections were left on the column drums and stone blocks, to make them easy to lift with ropes. Once the blocks were in place, the projections were chiselled off.

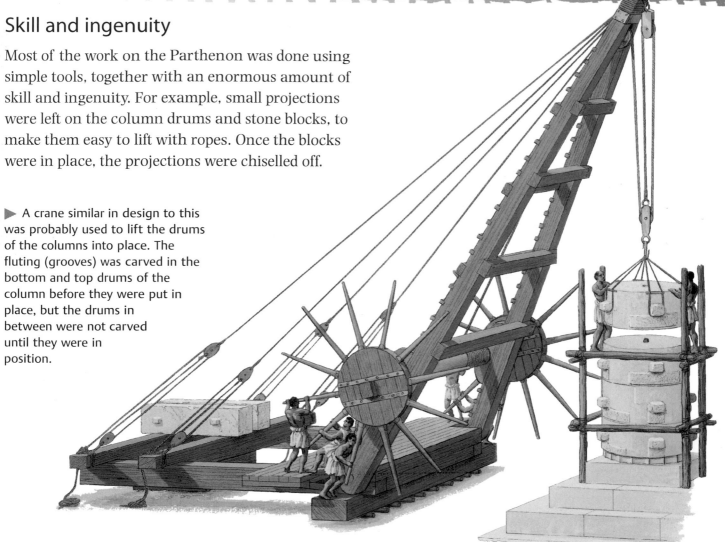

▶ A crane similar in design to this was probably used to lift the drums of the columns into place. The fluting (grooves) was carved in the bottom and top drums of the column before they were put in place, but the drums in between were not carved until they were in position.

Refinements

Phidias and his team went to tremendous lengths to make the Parthenon as perfect as possible. For example, they knew that if they made the steps leading up to the Parthenon perfectly level, to the eye it would look as if they sagged in the middle. So they built the steps with a very slight curve, rising a few centimetres towards the middle. Similarly, the columns of the outer colonnade bulged slightly, to make them appear absolutely straight to the eye. Such minute adjustments, sometimes as little as 1 millimetre, must have taken an enormous amount of work to achieve.

▼ The stone blocks used for the inner walls were levered into position as shown here. The metal ties holding the blocks together can also be seen.

A festival for Athena

By 402 BC, all the buildings of the Acropolis were completed. In that year, the annual summer celebrations to honour Athena were more joyous and splendid than ever before. The festival began with the Panathenaic Games (see page 52). These were similar to the famous Olympic Games, held every four years at Olympia.

The Panathenaic procession

After the Games came the festival proper. This began with a procession from the Diplyon Gate to the Acropolis. At the head of the procession were four young girls, carrying a new tunic (a *peplos*) for the ancient wooden statue of Athena. The procession began at the Diplyon Gate, and walked up the Panathenaic Way to the Acropolis.

▼ The Panathenaic procession arriving at the Acropolis. The procession included priestesses, hundreds of animals for sacrifice, musicians, important officials, chariots, horsemen, the winners of the Panathenaic Games, and most of the population of the city.

Government

Before the 5th century BC, Athenians had been ruled by tyrants, and they grew to hate the rule of one person over them. By the 5th century BC the city had therefore developed a democratic system of government that made it difficult for one individual to hold too much power. All important decisions were made at an assembly of citizens called the *ekklesia*. This met once every nine days or so, and at least 6000 people had to attend. Women and slaves were not allowed into the *ekklesia*.

▼ A view of the Agora looking west, as it might have looked in about 400 BC. The fountain house (see page 47), is in the foreground on the left. Top left is the platform of the Pnyx, where the assembly was held.

Key

1 Fountain house
2 South Stoa
3 Prison
4 Pnyx
5 Meeting place of the *boule* (see p. 42)
6 Temple of Hephaestus
7 Stoa of Zeus
8 Royal Stoa
9 Panathenaic Way
10 Painted Stoa
11 Shops
12 & 13 Law courts

The Agora

The Agora was an open area surrounded by shops and public buildings. The law courts and the prison were there, and other government buildings. The Agora itself was crowded with market stalls, and surrounded by shops and workshops.

Each morning, women came to the Agora to get water and exchange news. Later in the day, men gathered in the long, open-sided buildings (*stoas*) to hold discussions, do business or just chat. Meetings of the *ekklesia* initially took place in the Agora. Later, the meetings moved to the Pnyx, a hill near the Agora.

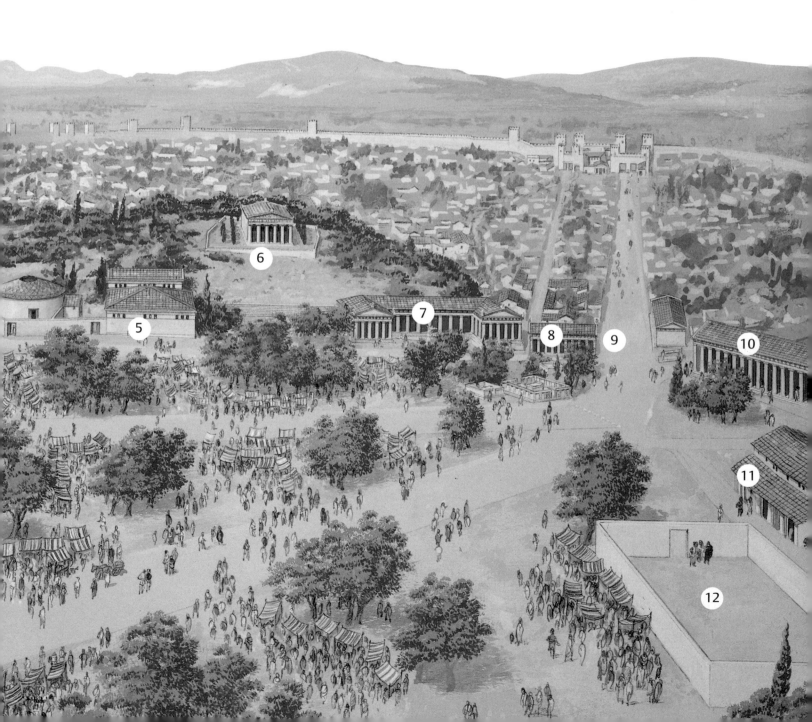

▲ Only 50 *boule* members were on duty at any one time. They met in one of the two buildings on the right in this picture. The round building on the left is the Tholos, where active *boule* members could eat at public expense.

Towards democracy

In the 7th century BC a group of ten archons, or magistrates, ruled Athens. The archons were elected each year, but they were always aristocrats and landowners. Poorer citizens complained that they had no real power. In about 594 BC Solon, who was respected by landowners and poorer citizens alike, was elected archon. He made changes to the law which created a group of 500 citizens, called the *boule*. They had the job of deciding what should be discussed at the full *ekklesia*. But soon tyrants once again took control of the city. Then in 508–507 BC the archon Cleisthenes reorganized the citizens into ten new tribes and laid the foundations of a truly democratic system.

▼ Only the foundations of the *boule* buildings have been found at the Agora. This photograph shows the site today.

Choosing by lot

But the archons that were elected each year were still usually aristocrats. It was not until 487 BC that a change was made. In that year, archons were not elected but were chosen by lot (at random) from the list of candidates. This change allowed people who were not rich landowners to become archons.

The *ekklesia*

From what we know about meetings of the *ekklesia*, we can guess that it was not always easy to get enough people to attend. Before each meeting, officials would stretch a long rope covered with red powder across the end of the Agora. They then used the rope to drive citizens towards the assembly platform. Any man found outside the assembly with red marks on his clothes could be punished. Speakers at the *ekklesia* spoke from a raised platform, but anyone could express an opinion. Voting was done by a simple show of hands.

▲ Although Athens was a democracy, strong personalities could still influence the *ekklesia*. The general and statesman Pericles persuaded Athenians to rebuild the temples of the Acropolis, using money from the treasury.

▼ Voting at the *ekklesia*.

Law and order

Athenians had a strong sense of fair play, and had a well-developed system of law courts. Most lawbreakers were tried in a court called the Helaia, but murderers were usually tried by a group of ex-archons called the Council of the Areopagus. In all trials, a jury made the decision as to whether the person on trial was guilty or innocent. They did this by a vote, using small metal tokens called ballots. By the 4th century BC Athenian juries were huge – 201 jurors were needed to decide even the smallest crime, and there could be as many as 2001. The odd number was to avoid an even split in the vote.

Punishment

Prison was not the most common way of punishing wrong-doers in Athens. Criminals might be fined or have their property taken, or they could be exiled (forced to leave Athens). Murderers were usually executed. Slaves were whipped or branded for crimes. The only people put in prison for crimes were foreigners, or criminals awaiting execution.

▼ Socrates was sentenced to die by poisoning. One of these medicine bottles found at the prison could have held the hemlock used to poison him.

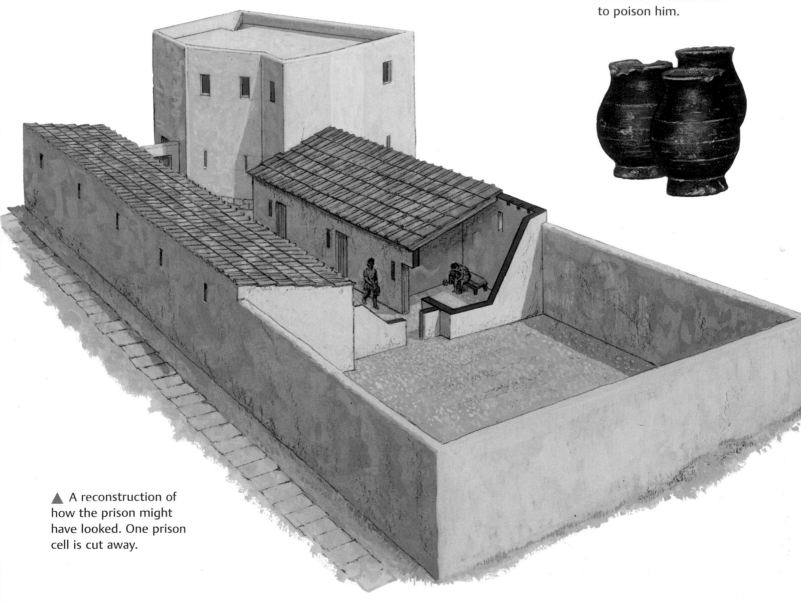

▲ A reconstruction of how the prison might have looked. One prison cell is cut away.

Ostracism

An unusual form of punishment was ostracism. Anyone whose behaviour was believed to be a threat to democracy could be ostracized: they would have to leave Athens for 10 years, within ten days of the decision being taken. A meeting of the full *ekklesia* was needed to ostracize someone, as more than 6000 people had to vote for it.

◀ Votes to ostracize someone were scratched on pieces of pot. This pot has the name Themistocles on it. We know that Themistocles was in fact ostracized.

The trial of Socrates

One Athenian trial that we know a lot about was that of the philosopher Socrates, because Socrates's friend and pupil Plato wrote an account of it. Socrates was accused of failing to worship the Athenian gods, and of introducing new religious practices. The trial was long and involved, but Socrates was eventually found guilty. He would probably have been sentenced to exile, but he refused to agree to leave the city he loved. He was therefore sentenced to death. He was held in the prison until the day of his execution. He was then given a poison called hemlock to drink.

▼ This painting by the French artist Jacques David is his idea of how Socrates might have died. It was painted over 2000 years after the event.

Work

The state of Athens included the countryside around the city as well as Athens itself. Most Athenians worked on land, raising animals or growing crops. The richest landowners had slaves to work their lands and managers to run their farms. They could afford to live in the city. The poorest farmers could barely get enough from the land to survive. But religious festivals and games gave even poor Athenians the chance to eat well and have a good time.

▼ This terracotta statuette shows a farmer ploughing. The plough is pulled by two oxen. Poorer farmers had to plough their land by hand.

Food

Farmlands around Athens were not very fertile. Few farmers could grow cereals such as wheat for bread. Sheep and goats were common animals, but it was difficult to raise cattle. Barley, olives, grapes and various types of bean were common food crops. Olives were also pressed to make olive oil.

By the 5th century BC the population of Athens may have been as high as half a million, including foreigners and slaves. The farmlands around the city could not feed this many people. Athenians had to rely on trading such products as silver, wine, olive oil and pottery to buy extra wheat grain.

▲ A cutaway of the fountain house as it might have looked in the 5th century BC. At one end was a basin from which water could be taken by dipping. At the other end were several spouts from which water ran continuously.

▼ One of the clay pipes used for water (right). The illustration on the left shows how the pipes fitted together.

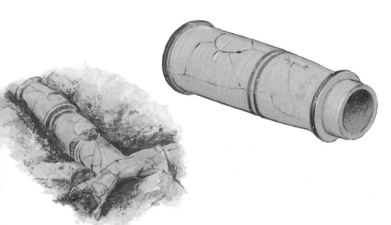

Water

Most houses in Athens collected rainwater in a tank or a well, but at some times of year this was not enough. From the mid-6th century BC, water from the mountains was brought to the city through a system of channels cut in the rock and clay pipes. The water fed several fountains in the fountain house at the south-east corner of the Agora. The women of a family usually collected water, although richer households had slaves to do this. Excess water flowed away in underground drains.

► This beautiful Athenian vase shows people picking olives. Athenian vase paintings were superb. Many examples have survived to the present day, and much of what we know about everyday life in ancient Greece comes from them. This vase has black figures on a red background; other vases had red figures on a black background.

► The head of a bronze statue of Athena. Bronze statues were made by casting the metal in a clay mould. Large statues were made in several pieces and then joined by brazing (a kind of welding).

Workshops and factories

Athens was famous for the skill of its craftspeople. Painters, potters, metalworkers, carpenters and leather workers were among those who had workshops and factories in the city. Pottery was used for storage vessels of all kinds, and for other objects such as cookers, grills and baths. Athenian pottery was sold throughout the Mediterranean. Most potters had their workshops in an area called the Kerameikos (the English word 'ceramic', which means pottery, comes from this word).

Around the Temple of Hephaestus there were many metalworkers, making objects in gold, silver, bronze and iron. Greek furnaces were not hot enough to melt iron, but blacksmiths could work the iron by beating it while it was hot. Paintings on vases also show carpenters and leather workers, but their work has not survived.

Shops and money

The Agora was the main shopping centre in Athens. There were shops around the edge of the Agora, and workshops where craftspeople sold their products directly. But most shopkeepers had stalls in the Agora itself. As well as craftspeople displaying their wares, there were farmers selling food, wine and oil, and merchants selling all kinds of goods, including products brought in from abroad. Inspectors went around the shops and stalls, checking that trading was fair. They carried standard weights and measures, which they used to make sure that shopkeepers were not cheating their customers.

▲ This vase painting shows a cobbler working at his bench.

▼ A two-drachma coin from the 5th century BC. The currency of Greece today is still called the drachma.

Social life

Athenian men spent most of their free time out and about, perhaps exercising at the gymnasium or chatting with friends in the Agora. Women spent their time at home, or visiting friends' houses. Their main chances to get out were to take part in religious festivals.

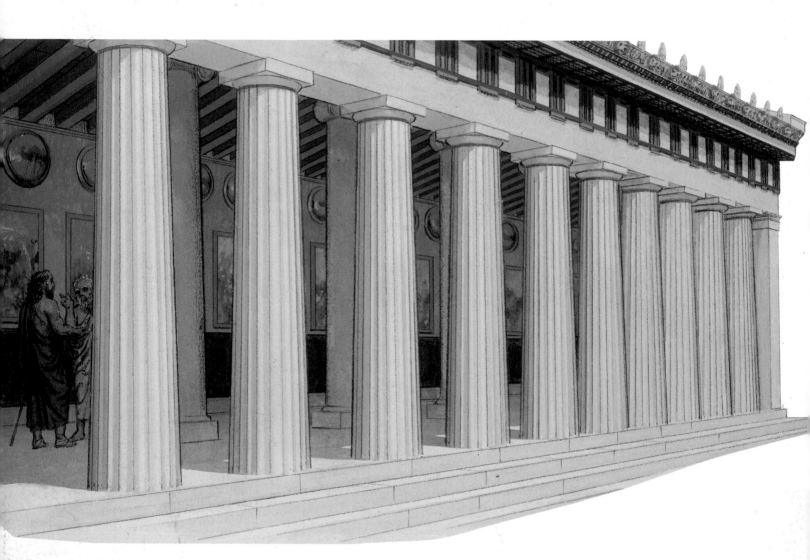

▼ A reconstruction of the Painted Stoa, one of the open-fronted, covered buildings in the Agora. The *stoas* were popular meeting places for Athenian men.

Staying at home

Men spent their free time during the day at the gymnasium or the Agora. But at night they would often be invited to a friend's house for a dinner party. All the guests at the meal would be men. The food was usually quite simple, even in rich homes – lentil or bean soup, with cheese, olives, garlic and plenty of bread. After the meal the guests would sing a hymn to Dionysus, the god of wine. Then the wineskin would be passed round, and the drinking began. Often there would be dancers, musicians and acrobats to entertain the guests. Such dinner parties could go on all night.

▶ At an Athenian dinner party the guests sit around the outside of the *andron* on couches, eating from small tables in front of them. They drink wine from shallow, double-handled bowls. A musician in the centre of the room is playing a double flute (a *diaulos*).

Going out

Women did not even do the shopping in Athens. So fetching water from the fountain in the Agora was a good opportunity for women to meet and chat. Richer women would have slaves to fetch water. If they wanted company they could visit a friend or relation. Women also held all-female dinner parties. But the main chance women had to go out was at religious festivals. Women took part in the processions and sacrifices, and some women became priestesses. The festival of Dionysus, held each March, was especially popular with women.

▼ This painting shows a group of women dancing, playing music and pouring offerings of wine at the festival of Dionysus.

Sports and games

There were 70 public holidays in Athens every year, most of them religious festivals. At most of these celebrations there were sports and other competitions. The biggest sports event in Athens was the Panathenaic Games, which was held every four years. These games were only open to men: married women were not allowed even to watch.

▼ The paintings on this bowl show three events from the pentathlon – wrestling, javelin and discus. The picks shown in the picture were used to soften the ground before a wrestling bout. As in all sports events, the men competed naked.

Running

For the Panathenaic Games, wooden stands were built on either side of a running track that ran down the centre of the Agora. The running events were run over various distances, as they are today. The first event, and the most important, was the sprint, which was run over a distance of about 184 metres. Next came a long-distance race which could be between 3½ and 4½ kilometres long. The third event was a middle-distance race of just over a kilometre. There were also other types of running race, such as a race in full armour.

Prizes for the winners depended on the games. At the Panathenaic Games, winners were given amphorae full of olive oil, which they could sell.

The pentathlon

The pentathlon was a real test of an athlete's all-round ability. There were five different events: throwing the discus, long jump, sprint, javelin-throwing and wrestling. The competitor who did best overall was the winner. The javelin used in these competitions was a light one made of wood. The athletes used a leather throwing strap to make the javelin spin in the air. In the long jump, competitors held weights in each hand as they jumped. Vase paintings suggest they swung them forward as they jumped. They may have then thrown the weights backwards to give them a longer jump.

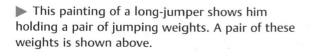

▶ This painting of a long-jumper shows him holding a pair of jumping weights. A pair of these weights is shown above.

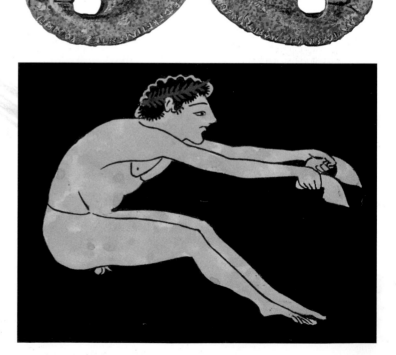

Wrestling and boxing

There were two kinds of wrestling competition in ancient Greece. In one, the aim was to throw the other wrestler to the ground – the winner was the first to get three falls. The other kind was all-in wrestling. Almost anything was allowed in this event. It went on until one of the wrestlers gave in.

Boxing was more dangerous than wrestling. The boxers did not wear padded gloves as they do today. Contests went on until one of the boxers was knocked out, which could take hours. Sometimes boxers were even killed. If this happened, the winning boxer was banned for life from those games.

▶ A statue of a boxer, by the sculptor Apollodorus. Although they did not wear padded gloves, boxers did bind their hands and wrists with leather thongs.

▼ The charioteer in this four-horse chariot is the legendary character Pelops, with his wife Hippodamia.

▲ This section from the frieze on the Parthenon shows horsemen riding in the Panathenaic procession. The section on the right shows how the frieze might have looked in the 5th century BC, when it was originally painted.

Horse races

Competitions on horseback were also part of most sports events. On the fourth day of the Panathenaic Games there were horse races on a stretch of open ground outside the city. As well as races on horseback, there were tests of skill, such as javelin-throwing from a horse. There were also chariot races for two- and four-horse chariots. Chariot racing could be as dangerous as boxing. The playwright Sophocles describes a race in which one competitor, Orestes, is dragged along the ground by his horses after his chariot breaks.

Carrying the torch

The final day of the Panathenaic Games ended with an all-night feast. At dawn there was a relay race carrying torches from the Academy, a gymnasium outside Athens, to the great altar of Athena on the Acropolis. Ten teams of runners, one from each of Athens' ten tribes, competed in the race. The winning team received 40 drachmas and a bull.

▶ A vase painting showing runners carrying torches.

Poetry and dancing

Unlike sports events today, Greek games included poetry, music, dancing and even a beauty contest! At the Panathenaic Games, poetry and music competitions were held on the first day. Poets competed to be best at reciting or singing extracts from the epic poet, Homer. Musicians played the lyre or the flute.

Competitions on the first four days of the Panathenaic Games were open, but events on the fifth day were limited to people from the ten tribes of Athens itself. There were contests to decide the best-looking and the strongest man. There was also a dancing contest, in which teams from each of the ten tribes performed a war dance with spears and shields. The winners in all these competitions received a prize of 100 drachmas and a bull.

▶ Two sides of a prize jar, or amphora, given to winners at the Panathenaic Games. They were filled with high-quality olive oil. Winners of some events received over 100 amphorae.

◀ Two musicians – a *cithara* player, and a player of the double flute or *diaulos*.

Music

The statesman Pericles built a large covered hall, called the Odeon, for musical events. There were competitions for boys and for men. Boys played a simple lyre or a single flute, while the men played a type of lyre called a *cithara*, or a double flute called a *diaulos*. As well as solo flute or lyre-playing, there were contests for singing while playing the lyre, and singing to accompaniment by a flute player.

▲ This painting, made in 1510 by the Italian painter Raphael, shows his idea of what the great Greek philosophers looked like. In the centre are Plato (left) and Aristotle. Sixth from Plato's left, with his back to Plato, is Socrates. On the left of the picture at the front is Pythagoras, sitting reading a book. In the crowd on the right, pointing at a slate on the floor, is Euclid.

Writers and thinkers

We do not know exactly what Greek music sounded like, because it was not written down. But Greek poetry and other writings have survived. The poetry of Homer was old even in the 5th century BC. He wrote about an earlier time, when Mycenae was the most powerful city in Greece. The historian Herodotus wrote about the war between Greece and Persia, while Thucydides wrote about the war between Athens and Sparta, from 431–404 BC.

The writings of Greece's great thinkers, or philosophers, have also survived. The word philosopher means 'love of wisdom'. Greek philosophers were interested in knowledge of all kinds. Philosophers such as Pythagoras and Euclid studied mathematics. Socrates and Plato were more interested in people's characters and their behaviour. Aristotle shared some of these interests, but he was also fascinated by the natural world.

The theatre

Every March, Athenians celebrated the festival of Dionysus, god of wine. On 10 March a wooden statue of the god was carried to the Temple of Dionysus on the slopes of the Acropolis. As usual, there were sacrifices, dancing, music and feasting. But one part of the celebrations was different from all other religious festivals. On the slopes just to the north of the temple, plays were performed – the world's first known theatre performances.

Plays all day

The plays were at first only small scenes within the general celebrations. But they were so popular that by 500 BC the performances had become a drama competition that lasted all day. Three playwrights were chosen to put on a set of four plays – three tragedies (dramas) and a light-hearted satyr play (satyrs were woodland gods that were half-animal, half-human). The plays were based on well-known stories of the time. Each playwright was sponsored by a rich Athenian, who paid for the actors, sets and costumes.

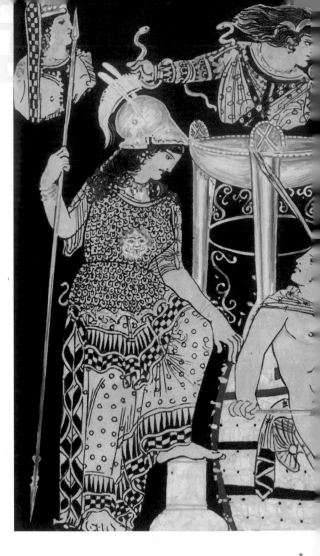

▲ A scene from a play by Aeschylus. Orestes kneels in the centre, with the gods Athena (left) and Apollo on either side.

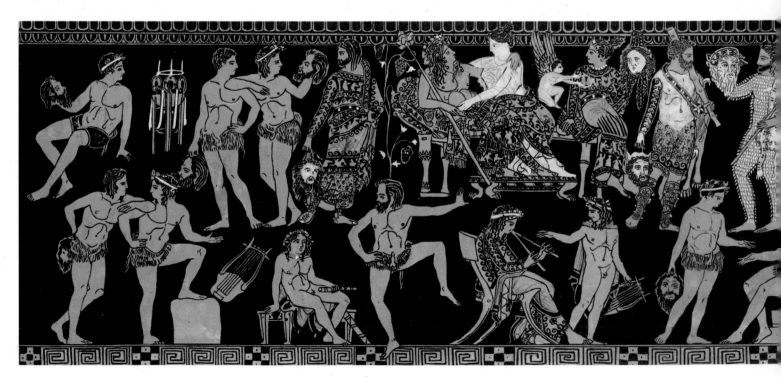

Playwrights

The greatest Athenian tragic playwrights were Aeschylus, Sophocles and Euripides. Some of their plays have survived and are still performed today. Aeschylus won the drama prize many times between 484 and 458 BC. Sophocles was younger than Aeschylus, and won his first contest in 468 BC, but he then dominated drama until his death in 406 BC. Euripides was Sophocles's main rival. He won his first competition in 441 BC.

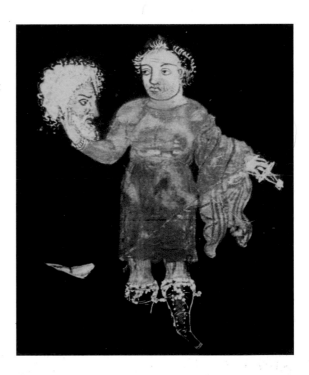

▶ A vase painting of an actor. Actors wore masks to help distinguish the different parts they played.

▼ A scene from a satyr play. At the top in the centre are the god Dionysus and his wife Ariadne.

Actors

Greek plays were performed by just three actors, one of whom did not usually speak. The actors were all men. In *The Libation Bearers*, a play by Aeschylus, the non-speaking actor surprises the audience by delivering a line near the end.

Most plays had many characters in them, so actors had to switch quickly from one part to another. In addition to the actors, the plays had a chorus. This was a group of men who all moved and spoke together. The chorus took one part in the play, but also commented on the action and on the other characters.

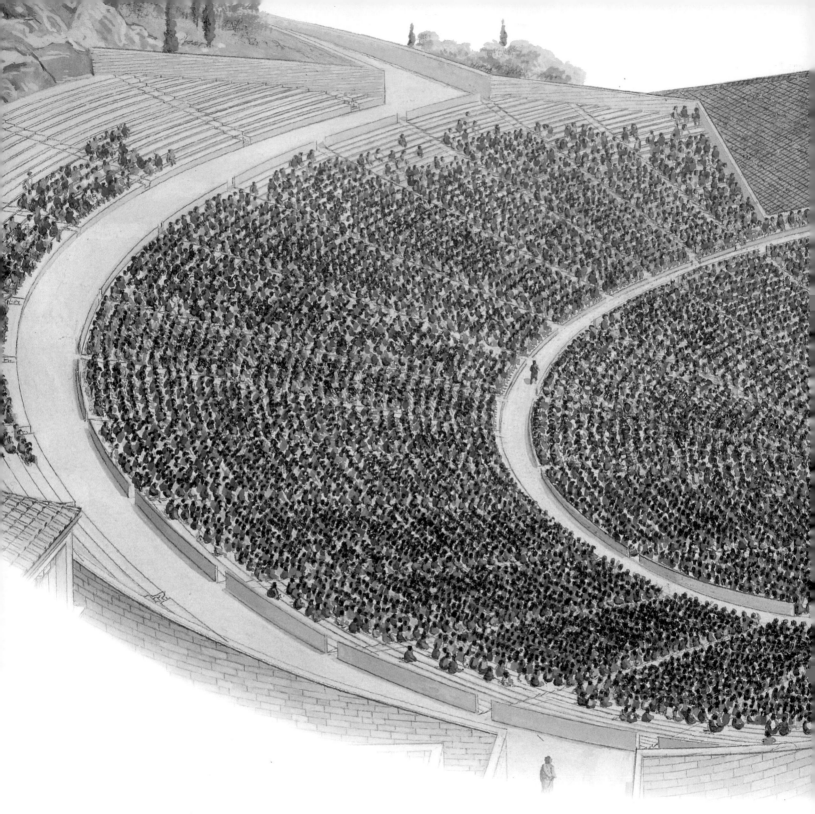

Comedies

From about 486 BC, comic plays were introduced into the festival of Dionysus. Actors wore padded costumes that gave them pot bellies and huge bottoms. These comedies made fun of politicians and other important people. The best of the Greek comedy writers was Aristophanes.

▲ A reconstruction of how the theatre in Athens might have looked in the 4th century BC. The theatre dwarfed the tiny Temple of Dionysus, the roof of which can be seen on the right. The large building behind the theatre is the Odeon, where music competitions were held.

Odeon

Temple of
Dionysus

Greek theatre

Greek theatres had a circular or semicircular space
for the actors. The audience originally sat on
wooden seating, but later the seats were made of
stone. Scenery was an important part of the plays.
It was hung in a wooden framework called a *skene*
(this is where the word 'scenery' came from).

▲ The early theatre was very simple, with a
circular stage area and no *skene*. The Temple
of Dionysus is bottom right.

61

Glossary

Acropolis: the steep-sided hill in the centre of Athens where the most important temples were built.

Agora: the large open area that was the main marketplace in Athens.

amphora (plural amphorae): a two-handled jar used in ancient Greece for storing and transporting wine, olive oil and many other things.

andron: the dining room in a Greek house.

archon: a chief magistrate or judge.

boule: a group of 500 Athenian citizens chosen each year to decide what should be discussed at the *ekklesia*.

cella: the inner room of a Greek temple.

chiton: a tunic. Women wore a long *chiton*, while the men's was shorter.

chlamys: a heavy woollen cloak worn by soldiers.

cithara: a stringed musical instrument, a type of lyre.

colonnade: a row of columns.

diaulos: a flute with two tubes, each played with one hand.

ekklesia: an assembly or meeting of all the citizens of Athens to make decisions about how the city should be run.

Erectheum: a temple on the Acropolis, dedicated to several different gods.

gymnasium (plural gymnasia): an open area where men could practice wrestling and other sports. There were three large gymnasia just outside Athens.

hemlock: a poison made from the hemlock plant.

himation: a large piece of woollen cloth worn as a cloak.

hoplite: a Greek foot-soldier.

lyre: a stringed musical instrument, a type of harp.

paidotribes: a schoolteacher.

Parthenon: the main temple on the Acropolis in Athens, dedicated to Athena.

pentathlon: an athletics competition involving five events. In ancient Greece these were throwing the discus, long jump, sprint, javelin and wrestling.

phalanx: a line of soldiers, the formation in which Greek hoplites fought.

philosopher: a thinker, someone who seeks after knowledge.

Pnyx: a hill near the Agora in Athens, where meetings of the *ekklesia* were held.

Propylaea: the entrance to the temple complex on the Acropolis.

satyr: a kind of woodland god, part animal and part human. In Greek satyr plays, the chorus were dressed as satyrs.

skene: the scenery for a play.

stoa: a roofed hall or walkway, where people met to talk or hear speeches.

ten tribes: the citizens of Athens were divided up into ten groups or tribes.

terracotta: a hard, unglazed type of pottery.

trireme: a type of Greek warship powered by three levels of rowers.

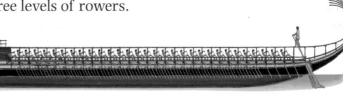

Index

Acknowledgements

The publishers would like to thank the following for permission to reproduce photographs.

Page 28bl AKG; 30tr Ancient Art and Architecture; 43tr, 45br, 46c AKG; 48 (all) Bridgeman Art Library; 49bl Athens National Museum; 57tc the art archive.
(b = bottom, t = top, c = centre, l = left, r = right)

All other photographs, illustrations and diagrams by Peter Connolly.